I'm Proud to Be Natural Me!™

Written and Illustrated by
Marlene Dillon

Edited by
Danielle Navonne

MDillon Designs & Publishing
CHICAGO

To Gorgeous
You will always be my special girl,
my favorite person in the whole wide world.

My name is _____,

and I'm proud to be natural me!

I'm Proud to Be Natural Me!™

Written and Illustrated by
Marlene Dillon

Edited by
Danielle Navonne

Some kids used to pick on me.

I'm proud to be natural me.

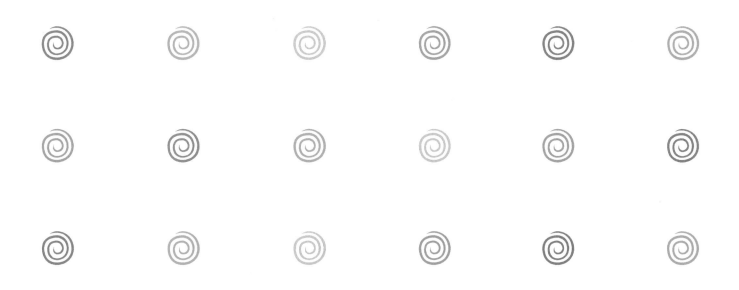

They said my hair was too kinky.

I'm proud to be natural me.

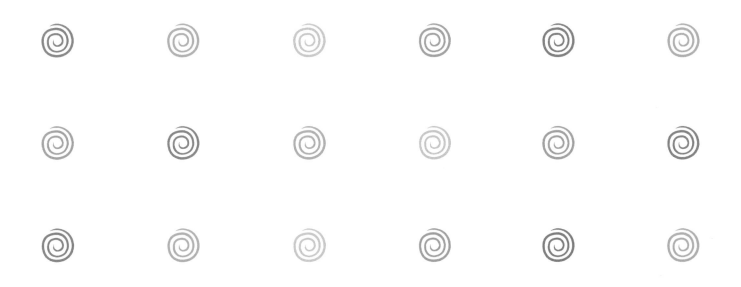

Others used to point at me,

I'm proud to be natural me.

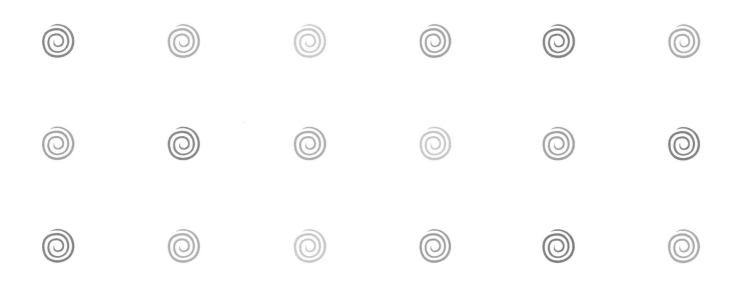

And said my hair was too nappy.

I'm proud to be natural me.

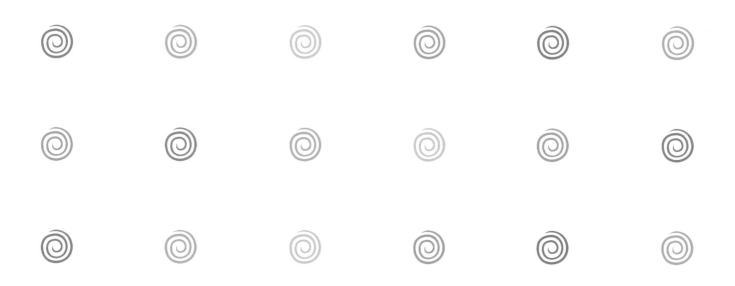

I told my mom and she told me,

I'm proud to be natural me.

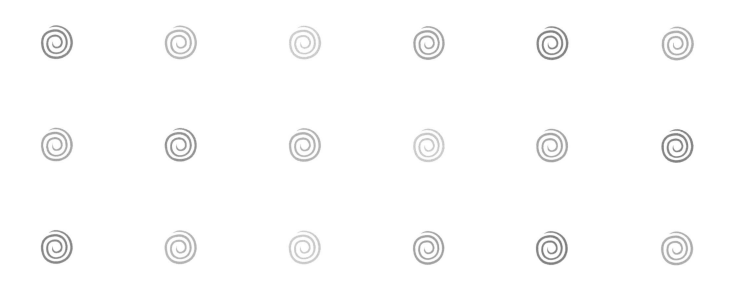

My hair is part of my beauty.

I'm proud to be natural me.

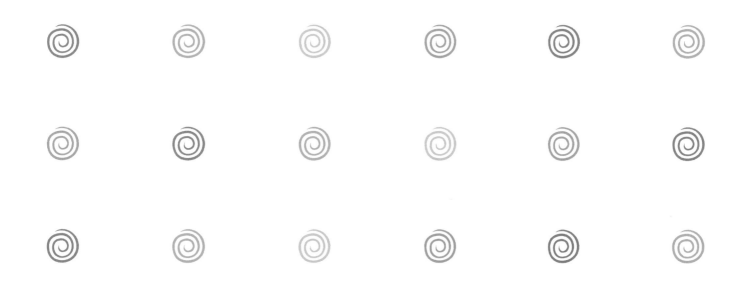

My tight curls are so pretty.

I'm proud to be natural me.

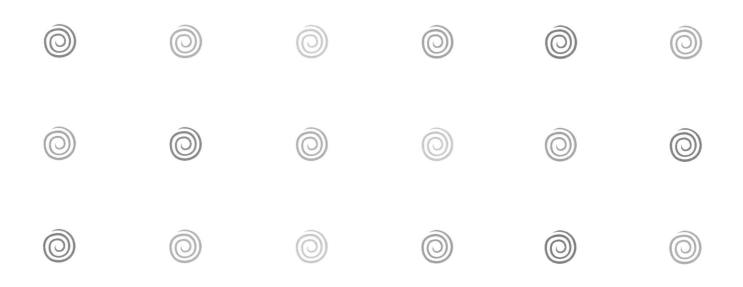

And that's how God created me.

I'm proud to be natural me.

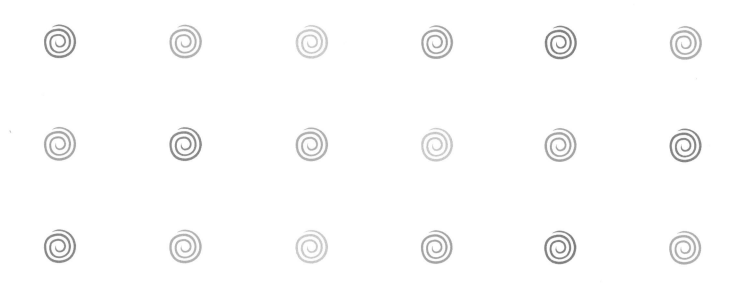

So now, their words do not hurt me.

I'm proud to be natural me.

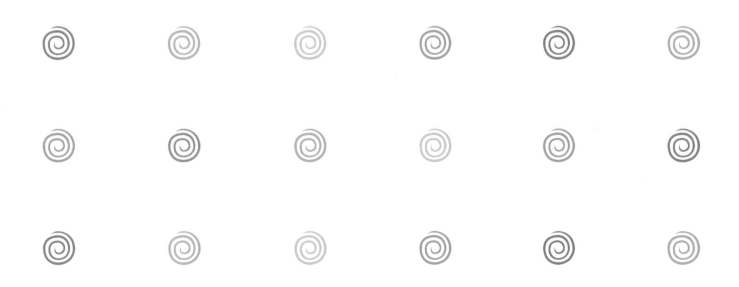

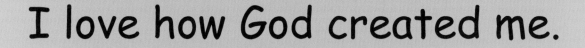

I love how God created me.

I'm proud to be natural me.

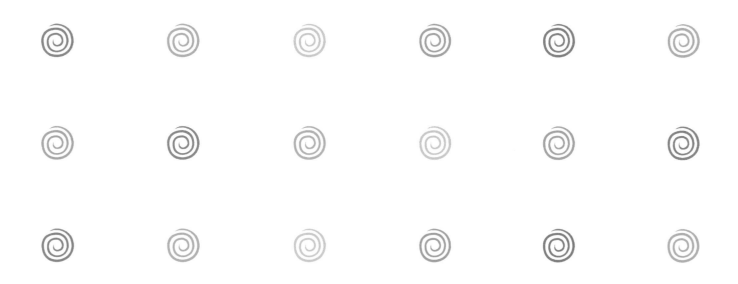

I've learned to LOVE what I see!

I'm proud to be natural me.

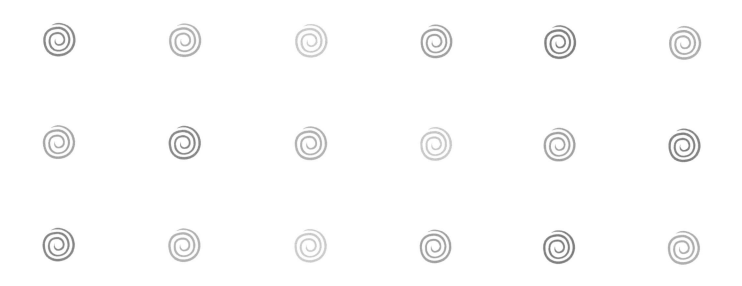

I've learned to LOVE what I see!

I'm Proud to Be Natural Me!

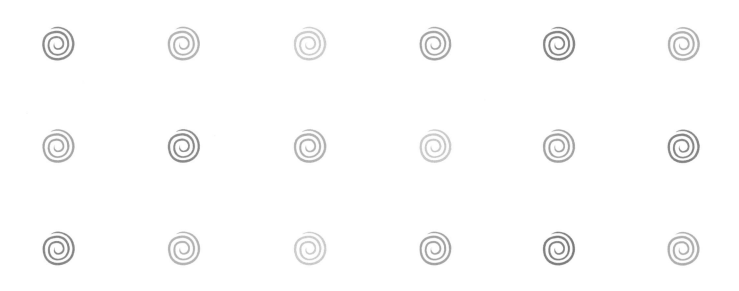

Write your own story.

_____

_____

_____

_____

_____

_____ .

E-mail your story to improudtobenaturalme@yahoo.com to receive a free autographed gift from author Marlene Dillon! Ask a parent to visit improudtobenaturalme.com for details! (While supplies last.)

Join our Fan Club!

Registration is easy and FREE!

improudtobenaturalme.com

Register your copy of I'm Proud to Be Natural Me!
and receive your official certificate of membership!

Explore. Share. Connect.

CPSIA information can be obtained at www.ICGtesting.com
Printed in the USA
LVIW01n2253070317
526480LV00002B/6